Rafale Saga

TO THE PEOPLE,

THOSE WHO INSPIRE US.

ACKNOWLEDGEMENT

Writing a book is harder than I thought and more rewardable than we expect the reward. None of this became possible without our friends and family they stood us during at every struggle done by us. We are eternally grateful to my college friends, who took in an extra mouth to feed when he didn't have to. They taught me discipline, tough love, manners, respect, and so much more that has helped me succeed in life. We truly have no idea where we had been they hadn't given us a roof over our head or became the father figure whom we desperately needed at that age.

Writing a book about Rafale is like to do social service which is like a surreal process. We found no words to express our sense of gratitude towards our parents for providing the necessary guidance and constant encouragement at every step of their endeavour. The pain taken by her for scrutiny of the rough draft as well as his valuable suggestions to plug the loopholes therein have not only helped me immensely in making this work see the light of the day but above all has helped in developing an analytical approach to this work.

We are extremely grateful to my respected teachers of the School of Law- Manipal University, Jaipur for their co-operation and guidance and their valuable time. I am highly indebted to the office and library staff of the college for the support in cooperation extended by them from time to time.

Having an idea and turning it into a book is as hard as it sounds. The experience is both internally challenging and rewarding. We especially want to thank the individuals that helped make this happen.

We want to thank our :

- Parents

- Teachers

- Grandma.

- All my brothers and sisters.

- My best friends

- Department of the court system for giving the judgement to us.

- We want to thank EVERYONE who ever said anything positive to me or taught me something. I heard it all, and it meant something.

- We want to thank God most of all because without God I wouldn't be able to do any of this.

Preface

Being a Law student makes us responsible for contributing towards this cause and enlightening people about, how Tax payer's money is being used by the country in enhancing their security.

The work contains a detailed analysis form the head to tail in a sequential way as the events unfolded and would help you get a broad overview of the subject matter.

We have not been Judge mental while expressing our views it's a decision which we have left for the reader to decide based on their prudence.

As stated by Jeremy Bentham **'greatest good for the greatest number'** We Hope the reader would keep the following in the mind before conclu**ding.**

Regards,

Siddhartha Kundoo & Saket Mangla

(Author)

Siddhartha Kundoo

Ph. No. +91 7424913711

siddharthakundoo5@gmail.com

https://m.facebook.com/MAVESID?ref=bookmarks

Saket Mangla

Ph. No. +91 9729466716

saket.mangla16@gmail.com

Contents

INDIA, FRANCE SIGN $8.9-BILLION
RAFALE DEAL FOR 36 FIGHTER JETS

Introduction

The Rafale is a propelled contender stage finished with lightweight-yet-solid composite materials. It is a twin-motor medium multi-job battle flying machine, made by French organization Dassault Aviation. The fifth era warrior has 'Omni job' ability to play out numerous activities at the same time, for example, terminating aerial rockets at an extremely low elevation, air-to-ground, and capture attempts. It has an Active Electronically-Scanned Array (AESA) radar framework in its nose. Outfitted with a wide scope of weaponry, the Rafale is expected to perform air matchless quality, ban ethereal surveillance, ground support, top to bottom strikes, hostile to deliver strikes and atomic prevention missions. The Fighter can take an interest in lasting "Fast Reaction Alert" (QRA)/air-safeguard/air sway missions, control projection and arrangements for outer missions, profound strike missions, air support for ground powers, surveillance missions, pilot preparing forays and atomic discouragement obligations. Rafale is the "notice kid" transformational contender which gives a route forward to The aviation based armed forces stood up to of doing "more" with "less", in a regularly changing vital and monetary condition.

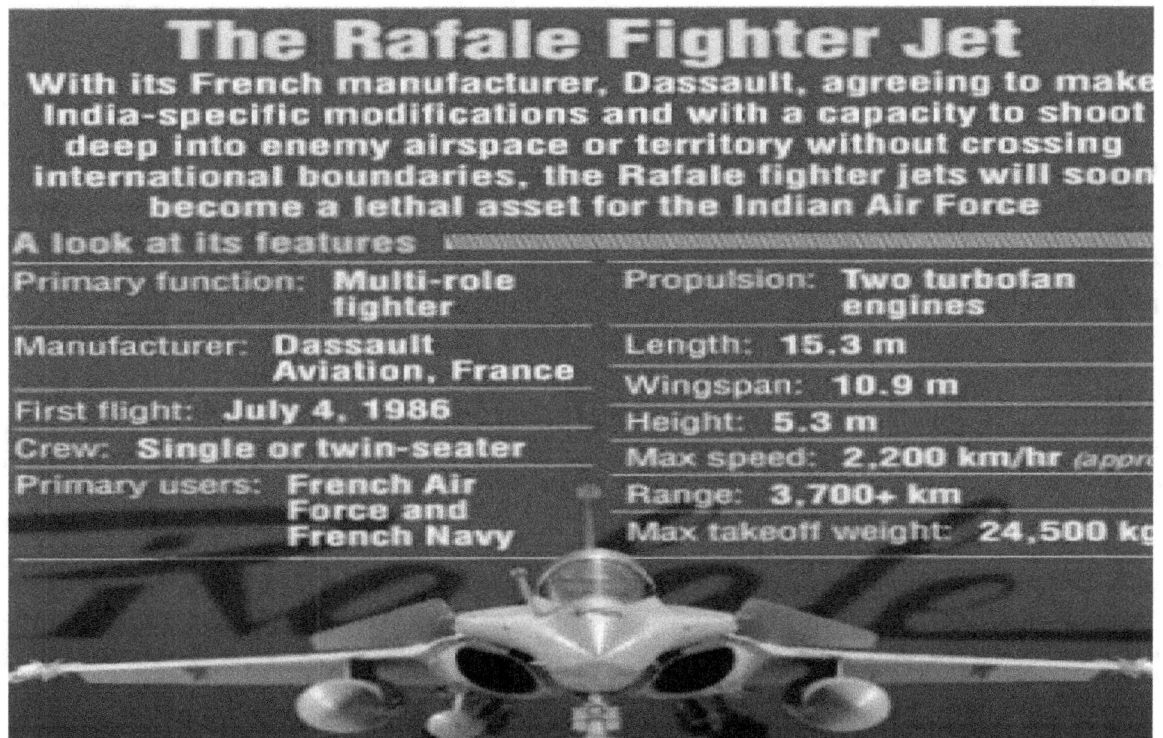

The Rafale Fighter Jet

With its French manufacturer, Dassault, agreeing to make India-specific modifications and with a capacity to shoot deep into enemy airspace or territory without crossing international boundaries, the Rafale fighter jets will soon become a lethal asset for the Indian Air Force

A look at its features

Primary function:	Multi-role fighter	Propulsion:	Two turbofan engines
Manufacturer:	Dassault Aviation, France	Length:	15.3 m
		Wingspan:	10.9 m
First flight:	July 4, 1986	Height:	5.3 m
Crew:	Single or twin-seater	Max speed:	2,200 km/hr (appr...
Primary users:	French Air Force and French Navy	Range:	3,700+ km
		Max takeoff weight:	24,500 kg

What led to the requirement of this fighter?

India is an emerging power. It has the world's 7th largest economy and is a growing superpower. It has enemies on its two fronts who happen to be all-weather friends.

Under such circumstances, the country needs to be extra conscious. For the two-front war, IAF needs 42 squadrons to defend the assets. The prime strategy of the IAF has always been based on the quality of aircraft rather than quantity. While IAF has around 650 Combat ready aircraft (Jets) compared to Pakistan's 400 and China's 1700. This disadvantage with China was bearable with the Superiority of IAF aircraft. To maintain quality superiority IAF needs the most technologically sophisticated 4++ Gen multirole aircraft.

Rafale was the best choice for IAF as proved during the trials.

Airship Portfolio

Air Superiority - Sukhoi 30MKI (2002), Mig 29 (1985, Now being moved up to SMT standard)

Multirole - Dassault Mirage 2000(1985, Now being moved up to Mk. 2 standards)

Interceptors - Mig 21 buffaloes (1964, Now being eliminated), HAL Tejas

Ground Attack - Mig 27, SEPECAT Jaguar

Presently, any decent top airforce on the planet might want to keep a solid blend of contender airship designs in their munitions stockpile. A multirole contender is equipped for playing out all jobs in a solitary bundle. Along these lines, you have many top AFs picking multirole aeroplane. Since Rafale suits the portfolio and Indians have a more joyful involvement in managing France over past safeguard bargains, Rafale was picked. (Predominantly because of specialized prevalence)

Likewise, the majority of the contenders aside from the Su 30 MKI can be viewed as old and of more seasoned frameworks than what is available today. Although they are being redesigned, still these airships are to be resigned in a not so distant future.

Why has India opted for Rafale?

Rafale was not India's solitary decision. A few worldwide avionics producers communicated enthusiasm after knowing the Indian government's mammoth intend to patch up its Indian Airforce armada by presenting MMRCAs.

Six eminent aeroplane producers contended to pack the agreement of 126 contender planes, which was touted to be the biggest ever protection obtainment arrangement of India.

The Initial bidders were Lockheed Martin's F-16s, Boeing's F/A-18s, Eurofighter Typhoon, Russia's MiG-35, Sweden's Saab's Gripen and Rafale.

All flying machine was tried by the IAF and after a cautious investigation on the offers, two of them — Eurofighter and Rafale — were shortlisted. Dassault packed away the agreement to give 126 warrior planes, as it was the most minimal bidder and the airship was said to be anything but difficult to keep up.

Real History Of The Deal Is Not From 2001 But From Much Before

The current Rafale mess is a consequence of long visionless and rudderless control of aviation and resistance industry of this nation and its administration. This chaos has its foundations in long 4 decades residency from the 1960s to 2000.

Will go in a type of a course of events:

- **1955– 1965**

o 1958: the First clump of GNAT flying machines are enlisted.

o 1961: India purchases the first clump of Mig-21 from USSR which went as high as 1200.

o   1961: First super-sonic fly of Asia, indigenously created HAL HF-24 takes first flight.

o   1962: Indo-China war. Indian economy in shackles after the war.

- **1966– 1977**

O   1971: HF-24 Inducted and participates in '71 War. Zero Casualties. Faultless execution.

o   1977: First HAL altered GNAT called Ajeet accepted.

- **1978– 1988**

o   1978: BIGGEST BLUNDER STARTS, JAGUAR BOMBER SELECTED.

o   1981: FURTHER RESEARCH ON HF-24 TERMINATED ONCE AND FOR ALL IN Favor OF JAGUARS.

o   1982: MiG's nearby retirement age, IAF needs substitution. First Mirage-2000 request put of 2 Squadrons.

o 1984: ADA is framed and primer investigation of Indigenous contender was begun, in the interim HAL not restricted in regardless of having specialized know-how. Next Blunder.

- 1985: Orders for 50 Mig-29

- **1989– 2001:**

O   1993: First full subsidizing for LCA is discharged [after 10 years]

o   1998: SU-30 bargain fixed

o 1999: Nuclear test ban put all exploration on LCA going on in the US ceased and analysts were expelled. Assessed defer was 4– 5 years. Next Set back.

o   2001: First LCA experimental drill. In the interim Mig's have crossed their age, experiencing life augmentation. First MMRCA bargain imagined.

- **Henceforth, rest is known.**

- Too numerous eggs in a single bin: 1200 Mig-21 alone from USSR in name of kinship.

- No balance between research for aviation and airship buy Mig-21 and HF-24 shared normal timetable had there been a smaller number of Migs been acquired and lay cash spent on HF-24 and Ajeet's exploration, the whole situation would have been unique.

- Blatantly ending the whole HF-24 program notwithstanding researchers and specialists being sure of doing it in a matter of months. HF-24 was built upstage a war legend and a develop one it was executed and killed ruthlessly henceforth in this way we lost a whole biological system in a solitary blow.

- Not including HAL in starter phases of LCA and setting up new ADA in this way diminishing HAL into a permit maker and making ADA an amateur in airship development made a hotchpotch. Subsequently, a brilliant decade is lost because of poor basic leadership and arranging. HAL got maimed in these years from a sword to a negligible blade.

The UPA Government initiated the procurement process

As demanded by the air force in 2007, the then UPA government floated tenders for 126 MMRCA Medium Multi-Role Combat Aircraft and bids were received from Russia's Mig-35, Swedish SAAB JAS-39 Gripen, American Lockheed Martin's F-16, Super Hornet, Euro fighter Typhoon and Rafale. In 2011 IAF narrowed the focus on Rafale and Euro fighter Typhoon. By January 2012, IAF selected Rafale as a winner based on cost. Out of 126 aircraft, 18 were to be delivered flying condition and 108 were supposed to build in India by HAL based on a transfer of technology (TOT) by Dassault. In 2014 HAL and Dassault signed a work-share agreement.

The UPA government claimed that the price of one jet was Rs526 crore and Dassault was ready to meet the delivery timeline. The UPA deal included 7.28% of the contract value as bank guarantee. However, quality control of the Aircrafts proposed to be manufactured by HAL remained a point of concern for Dassault. The French were not willing to take the responsibility of quality control of 108 aircraft produced in India. The other contentious issue was cost escalation due to almost three time higher Man hour's requirement for producing the Aircraft by HAL vis-a-vis Dassault. At the time of relinquishing the office, UPA2 could not sign the deal.

NDA's Rafale Deal

In April 2014 NDA came to power and Prime Minister Modi visited France and on 28th March 2015. Mr Anil Ambani structure Reliance Defense Ltd structure and team up with Dassault Aviation. Amid the visit bargain for obtaining 36 Rafale Aircraft in fly-away condition was declared. As announced in media, the arrangement for 36 Rafale was approx. Rs.59000 crore which works out to roughly Rs1167 crore per aeroplane. The NDA bargain supplanted the UPA's Sovereign assurance from the French government with Letter of solace. The solace letter issued by the French government is anything but a lawfully restricting archive in legitimate continuing. Moreover, the NDA bargain additionally was without the arrangement of a bank ensure, TOT and hostile to defilement condition. In October 2016, as a major aspect of the concession to balance condition, Dassault aeronautics and Reliance Defense Ltd, another organization in-flight part, reported their joint endeavour.

All Defense acquisitions in India are done under the terms of DPP-2013. The Standard Clauses for any guard Contract are referenced in Enclosure 8 of DPP-2013. This has segments on punishments for the utilization of undue impact, a trustworthiness settlement, specialists/organization commission and Access to a book of records and so forth.

Despite the DPP expressing Especially that the Standard Contract Document "would be the rule for all acquisitions", the Indian government expelled those provisions from the agreement for a buy of 36 Aircraft. The arrangement for Escrow Account for making instalment for the buy was likewise excluded. The escrow operator has the obligation to legitimately represent the escrow reserves and guarantee that use of assets was expressly for the reason proposed yet a tremendous sum was paid as development.

The Hindu guaranteed that the Modi government had consented to "drop" essential arrangements in the between administrative understanding (IGA) among India and France, including arrangements for hostile to debasement punishments and setting up of an escrow record to process instalments, in a matter of seconds before the arrangement was marked in 2016. It was likewise announced that Dassault Aviation had a bonanza by stacking the expense of India explicit Enhancements on 36 Aircraft rather than 126 No. It was likewise detailed that 'parallel arrangements' were completed by the PMO, undermining the endeavours of the Indian arranging group.

Offsets

To comprehend the balances clear we have to get the one certainty clear

"DASSAULT ALONE DOES NOT MAKE ENTIRE AIRCRAFT"

The pic above demonstrates how various organizations are involved in the whole Rafale Jet.

The real organizations are:

- **Dassault**

- **MBDA**

- **Rheinmetall**

- **Snecma**

- **Thales**

So if someone says Dassault and Reliance plundered us, Sorry to state that neither even Dassault nor Reliance won't get the chance to eat the total pie it must be appropriated as needs be with the different big deal then a large number of MSMEs included on Indian sides.

Presently there are the Indian offset accomplices:

*OEM= Original Equipment Manufacturer

*IOP= Indian Offset Partner

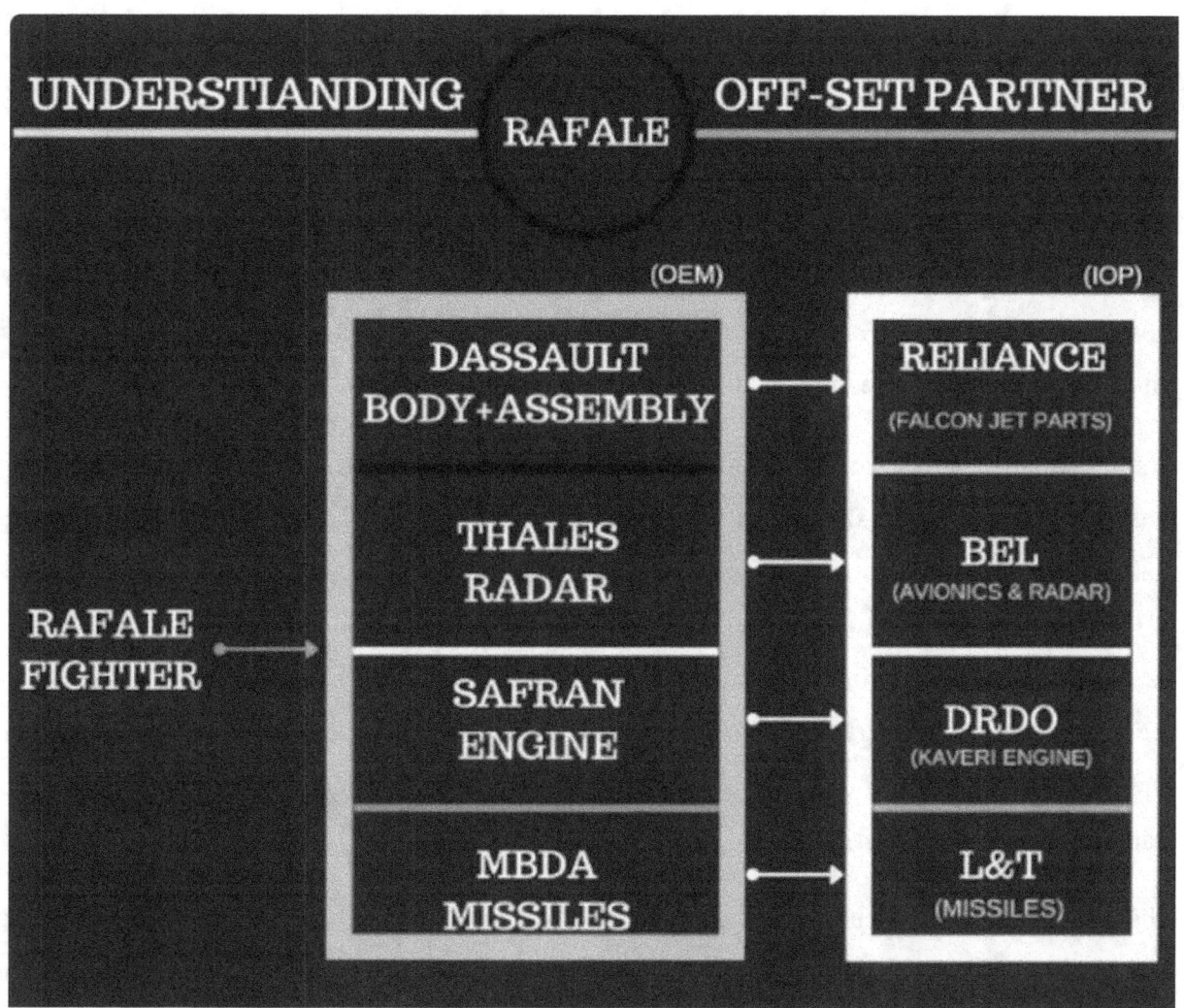

The entry of the Supreme Court

The first writ petition that is Writ Petition (Criminal) No.225 of 2018 on the NDA,s deal was filed by **Shri Manohar Lal Sharma**, a practising lawyer of the Court. The Petitioner pleaded the Court to register FIR against the deal and a Court Monitored Investigation. The Petitioner also sought relief for quashing the Intergovernmental Agreement of 2016 related to the purchase of 36 Rafale Jets.

Writ Petition (Civil) No.1205 of 2018 was also filed by Shri **Vineet Dhanda** claiming to be a public-spirited Indian. The petitioner stated that he was inspired to file the writ petition as he got agitated over the matter based on the newspaper articles.

The third writ petition bearing Writ Petition (Criminal) No.297 of 2018 was filed by **Shri Sanjay Singh**, a Member of Parliament alleging illegality and no- transparency in the procurement process. The said writ petition seeks investigation into the reasons for cancellation of earlier deal and scrutiny of the Court into the alteration of pricing and how a 'novice' company i.e. Reliance Defence replace HAL as the Offset partner. Cancellation of Inter-Governmental Agreement and registration of the FIR had also been prayed for.

The fourth and the last writ petition bearing Writ Petition (Criminal) No.298 of 2018 was filed by **Shri Yashwant Sinha, Shri Arun Shourie and Shri Prashant Bhushan** claiming to be public-spirited Indians. They were aggrieved by no registration of FIR by the CBI under a complaint made by them on 4th October 2018 which according to the petitioners, disclose a prima facie evidence of the commission of a cognizable offence under the provisions of the Prevention of Corruption Act, 1988. The prayer, inter alia, requested direction for registration of FIR and investigation of the same and submitting periodic status reports to the Court.

The Rafale aircraft procurement case reached the Supreme court after four Public Interest Litigations were filed. The Supreme Court observed that the scrutiny of the case will have to be made keeping in mind the confines of national security, the subject of the procurement being crucial to the Nation's sovereignty. Adopting such an approach, on 10th October 2018' when the first two writ petitions were initially listed before the Court, the Court had specifically observed in its order that it is proceeding in the matter by requiring the Government of India to apprise the Court of the details of the steps taken in the decision-making process. It was also made clear that the issue of pricing or matters relating to technical suitability of the equipment would not be gone into by the Court. The requisite information was required to be placed before the Court by the Government of India in a sealed cover.

The information which has been laid before the Court, which could be legitimately be brought into the public domain, be also made available to the petitioners or their counsels. Details about the induction of the Indian Offset Partner (IOP), if any, were also required to be disclosed. The Court also directed that the details about pricing; the advantages thereof, if any, should also be submitted to the Court in a sealed cover. In the backdrop of the above facts and somewhat constricted power of judicial review that the court held, proceed to scrutinise the controversy raised in the writ petitions

Adopting such an approach, on 10th October 2018 when the first two writ petitions were initially listed before the Court, the Court had specifically observed in its order that it was proceeding in the matter by requiring the Government of India to apprise the Court of the details of the steps taken in the decision-making process even though the averments in the writ petitions were inadequate and deficient. The Court had also indicated that it was so proceeding in the matter to satisfy itself of the correctness of the decision-making process. It was also made clear that the issue of pricing or matters relating to technical suitability of the equipment would not be gone into by the Court. The requisite information was required to be placed before the Court by the Government of India in a sealed cover. Before the next date of hearing fixed i.e. 31st October 2018, the other two writ petitions came to be filed.

The court studied the material carefully. They also had the benefit of interacting with senior Air Force Officers who answered Court queries in respect of different aspects, including that of the acquisition process and pricing. They were satisfied that there was no occasion to doubt the process, and even if minor deviations had occurred, that would not result in either setting aside the contract or requiring a detailed scrutiny by the Court. They had been informed that joint exercises had taken place and that there was a financial advantage to our nation. It could not be lost sight of that these were contracts of defence procurement which should be subject to a different degree and depth of judicial review. Broadly, the processes had been followed. The need for the aircraft was not in doubt. The quality of the aircraft was not in question. It was also a fact that the long negotiations for procurement of 126 MMRCAs had not produced any result, and merely conjecturing that the initial RFP could have resulted in a contract was of no use. The hard fact was that not only was the contract not coming forth but the negotiations had come practically to an end, resulting in a recall of the RFP. The wisdom of deciding to go in for the purchase of 36 aircraft in place of 126 doesn't merit judicial investigation. This was even though even before the withdrawal of RFP, an announcement came to be made in April 2015 about the decision to go in only for 36 aircraft. The country couldn't afford to be unprepared in a situation where the adversaries were stated to have acquired 5th Generation Aircrafts. It would not be correct for the Court to sit as an appellate authority to scrutinize each aspect of the process of acquisition.

The court also noted that the process was concluded for 36 Rafale fighter jet aircraft on 23rd September 2016. Nothing was called into question, then. It was only after the statement by the ex-President of France, Francois Hollande that petitions had been filed, questioning the aspect of the entire decision-making process and pricing. We do not consider it necessary to dwell further into this issue or to seek clause-by-clause compliances.

The challenge to the pricing of the aircraft, by the Petitioners, was sought to be made on the ground that there were huge escalations in costs, as per the material in public domain. The Court initially expressed its disinclination to even go into the issue of pricing. However, by a subsequent order, to satisfy the conscience of the Court, it was directed that details regarding the costs of the aircraft should also be placed in sealed covers before the Court.

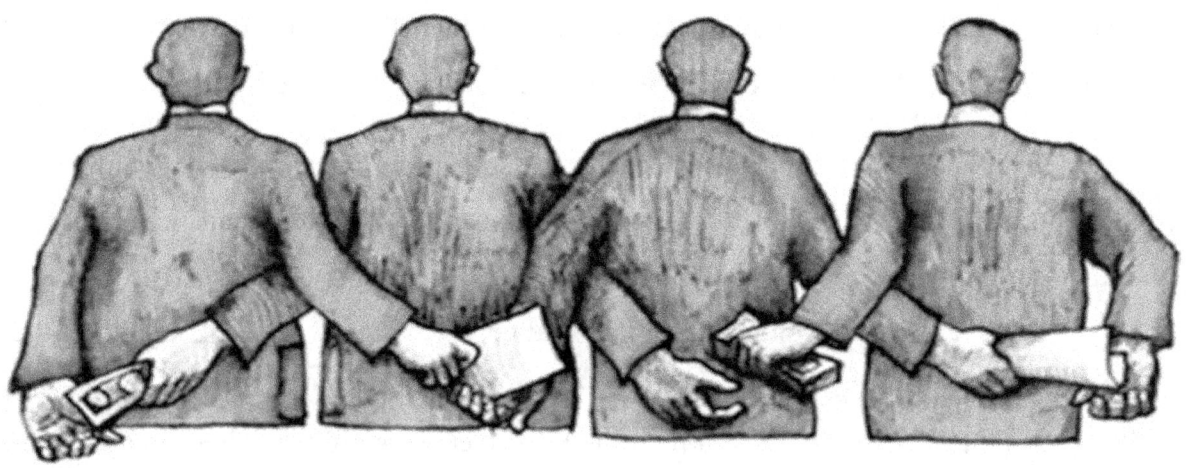

The most important CAG report which SC contradict its judgement

The material placed before the court showed that the Government had not disclosed pricing details, other than the Basic price of the aircraft, even to the Parliament, on the ground that sensitivity of pricing details could affect national security, apart from breaching the agreement between the two countries. The pricing details had, however, been shared with the Comptroller and Auditor General (hereinafter referred to as "CAG"), and the report of the CAG had been examined by the Public Accounts Committee (hereafter referred to as "PAC"). Only a redacted portion of the report was placed before the Parliament and was in public domain. The Chief of the Air Staff was stated to have communicated his reservation regarding the disclosure of the pricing details, including regarding the weaponry which could adversely affect national security. The pricing details were stated to be covered by Article 10 of the IGA between Government of India and Government of France, on purchase of Rafale Aircrafts, which protected classified information and material exchanged under the IGA governed by the provisions of the Security Agreement signed between both the Governments on 25th January 2008. Despite this reluctance, the material was placed before the Court to satisfy its conscience.

The court had examined closely the price details and comparison of the prices of the basic aircraft along with escalation costs as under the original RFP as well as under the IGA. The court had also gone through the explanatory note on the costing, item wise. Suffice to say that as per the price details, the official respondents claim that there was a commercial advantage in the purchase of 36 Rafale aircraft as compared to 126 Rafale Aircraft. The official respondents had claimed that there were certainly better terms in IGA w.r.t the maintenance and weapon package. The Court observed that it was certainly not its job to carry out a comparison of the pricing details in the subject matter. The court pricing details had to be kept in a confidential domain.

Fighter turns into voting Machine for General Election 2019

The Modi government was experiencing tension from the Opposition, all the more so after the misfortune looked by the BJP in three Hindi heartland conditions of Rajasthan, Madhya Pradesh and Chhattisgarh. The Congress wrested every one of the three states from the BJP.

The BJP was managing in Madhya Pradesh and Chhattisgarh for a long time and misfortune in these two states made a greater imprint in the Modi government's planning for re-appointment in 2019 Lok Sabha surveys.

The casting a ballot pattern in these three states demonstrated that the gathering might be on the course of losing 32 seats if the equivalent surveying design is rehashed in the Lok Sabha race.

Amid the crusade in a get-together race, Congress president Rahul Gandhi drove a frontal assault on the BJP charging defilement in Rafale bargain. Calling the India-France guard to bargain a Rs 58,000-crore trick, Rahul Gandhi blamed PM Modi for defilement.

In his decision discourses, Rahul Gandhi rehashed stated, "chowkidar chor hai [the watch is a thief]" alluding to Narendra Modi's survey battles in front of 2014 Lok Sabha surveys.

In those days, Modi had made claims of debasement against the Congress-drove UPA government his survey board promising that he would go about as a leader yet as a chowkidar (watch) to guarantee that no defilement happens in the legislature.

Rafale bargain had turned into the greatest spoil on the NDA government and individual picture of PM Narendra Modi. Rahul Gandhi had blamed him for marking the Rafale arrangement to profit representative Anil Ambani, whose Reliance Defence got a piece of the off-set arrangement with the Dassault Aviation, the creator of Rafale warrior stream.

The entire political portrayal worked by PM Modi and the BJP on hostile to defilement board was being supplanted with an elective that said that the Modi government was not neutralizing debasement but rather had enjoyed defilement.

The Supreme Court decision has given the BJP new ammo to hit back at its adversaries when it had endured the greatest misfortune since 2014 Lok Sabha race.

Rafale bargain was initially consulted with France amid the UPA government yet the arrangement couldn't take off. At the point when the BJP-drove NDA government came in power, PM Modi sped up the procedure at the most abnormal amount with the French government and got the arrangement marked in 2016.

As far back as the arrangement was finished for the buy of 36 Rafale contender flies, the Congress considered it a trick and propelled gigantic political crusade against the Modi government constraining it to issue a few elucidations.

A few activists and government officials moved the Supreme Court not long ago. The Supreme Court requested that the Modi government present the subtleties of the basic leadership process for Rafale bargain in a fixed envelope. In the wake of contemplating the administration's reaction, the Supreme Court had saved its request on November 14. The petitions were rejected on Friday.

The central government waived off critical provisions for anti-corruption penalties as well as overruled financial advisers' recommendations for making payments through an escrow account just days before it as escrow account is especially known as a financial safeguard but government waived that account and signed the inter-governmental agreement with France to get 36 Rafale jets.

The particular move will have significant implications on the Narendra Modi government which is due to fight in the Lok Sabha election later in the year as it has made eliminating corruption as one of its main planks for governance

government   the people

<u>Conclusion</u>

The Reliance Group was a piece of the Rafale bargain since 2012 and after that, it quit managing in protection creation. Dependence Group was at that point in barrier producing yet they were not accomplices in the Rafale bargain. They didn't hold any agreement or concurrence with both Government of India and Government of France. They were never chosen by any Government as one of the counterbalance accomplices. Every one of the announcements of Congress President Rahul Gandhi was refuted by Government of France, Prime pastor of France, Finance Minister of India, Defence Minister and numerous other people who were a piece of the Rafale Deal.

The Supreme Court would not structure an examination in the Rafale bargain, referring to the innate constraints of its capacity to attempt a legal survey of "delicate" resistance contracts and its absence of aptitude in investigating evaluating or specialized attainability. The move was invited by the legislature and denounced by its pundits. The seat driven by boss equity of India Ranjan Gogoi rejected requests to arrange a test into defilement charges. The court said "We are fulfilled that there is no event to truly question the procedure, and regardless of whether minor deviations have happened that would not result in either putting aside the agreement or requiring an itemized examination by the court," the seat said. "We discover no explanation behind any mediation on the touchy issue of procurement of 36 guards flying machine. View of people can't be the premise of an angling and meandering enquiry by this court, particularly in such issues."

www.ingramcontent.com/pod-product-compliance
Lightning Source LLC
Chambersburg PA
CBHW081548280526
45788CB00010B/3395